PRAISE FOR *THE JESUS MANIFESTO*

David Moffett-Moore brings the Sermon on the Mount, what he calls Jesus' Manifesto, to life for 21st Century Christians. That is, while these are expressive of God's kingdom, and are challenging, they are not reserved only for some future state. They speak to us in the here and now. In this study guide, which is rooted in sermons preached, groups and individuals both are allowed to delve deep into these words of Jesus so that they might be transformed by the encounter.

**– Dr. Bob Cornwall**
Pastor Central Woodward Christian Church, Troy, MI, author of
*Unfettered Spirit: Spiritual Gifts for the New Great Awakening*

If you are looking for an excellent resource for study of the Sermon on the Mount, look no further. David Moffett-Moore's *The Jesus Manifesto* is based on a solid Biblical foundation. Obviously, he has done his homework. There are also extremely practical illustrations from children's stories to science fiction films plus numerous personal experiences from his forty year ministry. Particularly helpful are the sets of questions at the end of each chapter: A Call to Reflection, A Call to Conversation, A Call to Action, and A Call to Prayer.

Central to the study is the claim that the church of the twenty-first century is more like the church of the first century than the church of the twentieth century. We also live in a time when everything is falling apart, the same kind of world Jesus addressed in these beloved teachings. Jesus said that this is how we are to live; David Moffett-Moore shows us what this means for us today. To the author's credit, he does not shy away from the controversial issues involved in Jesus' teachings on violence, justice and peace-making.

Along the way there are little gems like these: "Blessed = heaven's own happiness," and "Jesus invites us to resonance, where our lives reverberate with yearnings of God."

In short, David Moffett-Moore has made a good case that Jesus is a spiritual revolutionary and The Sermon on the Mount is his manifesto.

**Dr. David Cartwright**, Minister Emeritus at Hazelwood
Christian Church, Muncie, IN
Author of *Wounded by Truth – Healed by Love*

In changing tumultuous times, Dr. Moffett-Moore reminds us that we need a reflective return to the basic manifesto of a 1st Century rebel to find a renewed vision for following Jesus today. God is calling His Church to thrive in changing times with a proactive love for the world. Thanks, David, for what is a strong and fresh study on classic Christian truths. I'll be implementing this study at my church very soon!

**Dr. Chris Surber**, Director of Supply and Multiply
Ministry, Montrouis, Haiti, author of *Render Unto Caesar* and
*Gomorrah Was Religious Too*

David crawled into my soul and put on paper the truth I claim as my faith. In the midst of recent conflicts there were words of truth that, while challenging, brought comfort, hope, and restored joy. This book is about why the Beatitudes matter to our faith. This shows why Christians are called to service in the name of Jesus. David Moffett-Moore pulls out the secrets of our souls, our stress, our hurts, our frustrations, and gives us a plan: reflect, converse, act, and pray. We are not helpless. We do not have to sit down. We can go back to the heart of the Gospel and live freely, transforming the world and giving light, hope, and life. David put into words what our hearts have been trying to tell our heads.

— **Rev. Shauna Hyde**, pastor of First United Methodist
Church, Ravenswood, WV, author of *Vicar of Tent Town* and
*Fifty Shades of Grace*

# THE JESUS MANIFESTO

## A PARTICIPATORY STUDY GUIDE TO THE SERMON ON THE MOUNT

DAVID MOFFETT-MOORE

Energion Publications
Gonzales, Florida
2016

Cover Design: Henry E. Neufeld
Cover Image: Adobe Stock 89313185
Chapter Header Image: 86981325


ISBN10: 1-63199-228-7
ISBN13: 978-1-63199-228-5
Library of Congress Control Number: 2016938020


Energion Publications
P. O. Box 841
Gonzalez, FL 32560

energion.com
pubs@energion.com

# ACKNOWLEDGEMENTS

Every good thought has a thousand sources.

I thank my father for forty-three years of good and faithful service as a pastor, for preaching the word in season and out, and especially for the sermons I overheard when I was a rebellious child trying not to listen. I thank my mother for standing her ground and making sure I did listen. I thank the congregations that have endured my preaching over nearly forty years. I especially thank Portage United Church of Christ, where I currently serve, and for the careful response and reflection they provided during the summer of 2015 and my series on the Sermon on the Mount. It is a delight and an honor to serve with them in our common ministry.

I thank my wife Becki for supporting me throughout this process and for encouraging and tolerating me when the well ran dry and I grew frustrated. Without her motivation, this manuscript would still be waiting in my thumb drive. Thanks to Henry Neufeld of *Energion Publications* for providing the Participatory Bible Study Series as a venue for Bible studies that can be both provocative and practical in their orientation.

Lastly, thanks to the reader, without whom all this effort would be superfluous and meaningless. For what errors and shortcomings still exist in this little volume, I accept full responsibility and offer my humble apologies. In spite of its limitations, may you find it helpful and challenging in your spiritual pilgrimage.

# THE PARTICIPATORY STUDY SERIES

The Participatory Study Series from Energion Publications is designed around the motto "scholarship in service." Each guide is written by someone with a strong background in the topic studied and designed for use by lay people in Sunday School classes and small groups, as well as for individual study.

These guides are not all easy reading. Some of the topics covered require serious effort on the part of the student. But the guides do provide all the resources necessary for a fruitful study.

The section "Using this Book" is designed for the series but adapted to the particular study guide. Each author is free to emphasize different resources in the study, and to follow his or her own plan in presenting the material.

It is our prayer at Energion Publications that each study guide will lead you to a deeper understanding of your Christian faith.

— Henry Neufeld, General Editor

# Using This Book

This study guide is will be found very helpful for small groups, such as Sunday School classes. Individual students working on their own will benefit from the stimulation it provides. It might serve as an introductory textbook.

The book itself will give you with an overview of a topic, the Sermon on the Mount (Matthew 5-7), providing specific questions for discussion. There are several things you can do to make your study more profitable.

1.  Where **resources** are suggested, divide them between members of the class and consult them during your study time. Students can bring what they have learned to the class. This is also a good time to help your church improve its library. Suggest some of these resources for your library shelves.

2.  **Share.** The Participatory Study Guides to Bible books pioneered sharing as an integral part of your study, but it will work just as well when you are studying a topic. Sharing does not mean harassing other people with your viewpoint. It's a matter of listening and being accountable in your community. If you come to a conclusion, listen to others who can comment on it and possibly point out reasons that you may be wrong, or ideas that may not have occurred to you.

This topical guide in this series is exceptionally practical. Be sure to think of living the word as you learn it!

# TABLE OF CONTENTS

# CHAPTER I

## INFORMATION:
## WHY THIS? WHY NOW?

Why do we need another study of the Sermon on the Mount? What is different about this study? Why this study, and why now?

We all know we are living in changing, tumultuous times. Church attendance and membership are dropping precipitously. We can't say that our young adults are leaving the church. In truth, many of them were never really there in the first place. We are swamped with other choices for our dedicated Sunday mornings; Sunday at 11:00 A.M. is no longer the holy hour. We are surrounded with other priorities, loyalties and interests. People are satisfying the basic human need for interaction via the internet. The fastest growing religious segment is the "nones," those who have no religious preference.

Phyllis Tickle writes in *The Great Emergence* that we are having one of our "every five hundred years" garage sales. Phil Jenkins in *The Next Christendom* describes what he sees as a millennial transformation. We have titles like *Christianity for the Rest of Us, Why the Church Must Change or Die* and *The Church after Christianity.* It is clear that we are in the midst of a change that is larger than any of us can understand. I've said the church of the 21$^{st}$ century is more like the church of the 1$^{st}$ century than that of the 20$^{th}$ century.

Like then, we live in a world that is deeply divided, strongly segregated, with different parts of society not communicating with each other. Some are very passionate about their religion, willing to die or kill for it, for others religion is irrelevant.

The Book of Acts begins with Pentecost and Peter's first Christian sermon, converting three thousand in an instant. In Acts the church seems to go from one victory to another, but we know that Luke is leaving out quite a bit of history.

The Crucifixion took place around 30 C.E. In the Gospels, Peter, Andrew, James and John form Jesus' inner circle. We never hear from Andrew again. James is martyred in the 40s C.E. Peter is martyred in Rome in the 60s, along with Paul — who is the author or actor of half the New Testament, through his letters and his role in Acts. Of all the apostles, John is the only one traditionally to have died a natural death, around the end of the first century C.E. James, the brother of Jesus and leader of the Jerusalem church, is also martyred in the 60s. In its earliest decades, all the leaders of this foundling movement are executed by the Roman government.

In the late 60s there is an uprising in and around Jerusalem, an attempt to free the faith from pagan rule. From 70 to 73, Rome lays siege to Jerusalem and the city slowly starves. Any who comes out to surrender is publicly killed. Rome has had enough of these uppity, irritable Jews. The city is sacked, survivors executed. The temple is destroyed. First century Judaism is in crisis. The temple has been the only place where God may be worshiped in all the earth, the spot where God's presence is real. One thousand years of Jewish faith and practice is extinguished. How will Judaism survive? For many it doesn't; they move to other, more tolerant and tolerable religions or to no religion. The Jews of the Diaspora are less affected, but the entire population of Judah is in turmoil. Some find their way from temple to synagogue, from sacrifice to teaching. What we know as modern Judaism survives the labor pangs of this frightful birth.

Some are Messianic Jews, winning a surprising Gentile following with what they call "the True and Living Way." Messianic Jews who believe and have experienced Jesus to be their Messiah. What are these Jews who believe Jesus to be the Messiah to do with all their Gentile converts? How do they make Gentiles to be Christian Jews or Jewish Christians? Is there some other way to Jesus?

These early, nascent Christians — who are not so called or identified yet — are also surrounded by Greek, Gnostic, Roman,

Persian and Egyptian mystery cults and religions and philosophies. What "new thing" can they let in? What must they keep out? How are they to decide?

What does it mean to be a follower of Jesus in such a volatile environment? We have the motivation for the writing of Matthew. Historically, Matthew has been viewed as the "first" gospel. For centuries, Matthew was seen as the first one written, with Mark as a *Reader's Digest* version; now we know Mark was written first, Matthew and Luke both had a copy of Mark and the mysterious "Q" gospel, plus other resources. None were written by eyewitnesses, none by the names ascribed to them. Yet Matthew has been viewed as the most important, most influential, best suited for teaching, etc.

And the most Jewish. Matthew sees Jesus as the new Moses and styled his Gospel as five books, paralleling the five books of Moses. Moses went up the mountain to receive the Ten Commandments; Jesus went up the Mount for the Sermon and gave eight beatitudes. Not a perfect match, but we get the point.

Depending on translation, the Sermon on the Mount contains some two thousand words in five pages, barely enough for a magazine article. Yet it has had a huge historical impact. Augustine gave it the title of "Sermon on the Mount." Martin Luther finds key connections for his Reformation. Leo Tolstoy builds his mammoth *The Kingdom of God is Within You* upon it. Mahatma Gandhi, Dorothy Day and Martin Luther King Jr. all have their social witness inspired by its message.

In his *Daily Study Bible*, William Barclay writes 222 pages on the Sermon on the Mount. That is a page for every ten words in the Sermon, including the "of's," "the's" and "and's"!

John Adams, contributor to the *Declaration of Independence* and our second president, said, "The Ten Commandments and the Sermon on the Mount are my entire religion." Harry Truman, President in the middle of the 20th century who ordered the use of the atom bomb, said, "There is not a problem in the country or this world that could not be solved by the principles of the Sermon on the Mount." Dorothy Day, noted Catholic social worker and activist, declared, "Our entire manifesto is the Sermon on the Mount."

And that is what it is: a manifesto, a public declaration of motives and intentions. It is intended to be radical, "of the roots," extreme and intense, to be personal, practical and powerful. It declares, "This is how we are to live." "This is what it means to be Christian, to be followers the One who is the True and Living Way."

Written in or around Antioch in Syria, where they were first called "Christian," between 80 and 85 C.E. The old world was shattered, the new world was not yet seen. The old faith had vanished; something new was not yet seen.  The generation of eyewitnesses was disappearing; people needed something they could hang on to, something that would help hold them together in these violent, shocking times. They needed something to affirm, something that would *confirm* their faith. They believed they were called to a new world and to live in a new way; they needed a strong and clear declaration of that Way. In answer, the author of Matthew gives us this Jesus, not the historical flesh and blood Jesus of Nazareth, but the Jesus of the New Testament Church, the Jesus who is the new Moses, leading God's chosen to a Promised Land. If we climb this mount, we may yet see it, off in the distance: a vision and a calling.

## A CALL TO REFLECTION

What is your understanding of the historical Jesus? And of the original setting for the gospels? How is the writing of the gospels an expression of the early church speaking to and forming the early church?

## A CALL TO CONVERSATION

What has been the impact of the Sermon on the Mount in your life?

How do you describe your relationship with Christ today? How has it grown through your lifetime?

## A CALL TO ACTION

Where do you see the church under stress today? What can you do about it?

Where do you see the gospel making a difference in someone's life? What can you do to support it?

## A CALL TO PRAYER

God, remind us again that it is not enough for us to say our prayers or read our scriptures, if doing so makes no difference in our lives and the lives of others. Lord, use us to be your answer to someone else's prayer. For Jesus sake. Amen.

# CHAPTER 2

# BLESSED ARE, THEIRS IS

### Matthew 5:1-16

Matthew uses a very formal introduction to the Sermon, carefully describing each step as Jesus begins: seeing the crowds, ascending the mount, sitting down, disciples approaching, beginning to speak, opening his mouth, teaching them, saying. Almost everything but how many breaths Jesus took. This is a literary device to let us know that something important is about to take place and we had better pay attention, and applies to the entire sermon, which ends with 7:28-29, "When Jesus had finished saying these things, the crowds were astounded at his teaching, for he taught them as one having authority, not as their scribes." The Sermon on the Mount is intended to describe essential Christianity, the essence of what it means to follow Jesus.

With the Beatitudes we have a common rabbinical form of teaching, something with which all the Jewish Christians would be comfortable. There are Beatitudes scattered throughout the Bible. Each of these eight Beatitudes are worthy of a sermon. Luke's "Sermon on the Plain," Luke 6: 17-49, which includes much of Matthew's Sermon on the Mount, includes only three beatitudes. Unlike Matthew, Luke balances each blessing with a woe: Blessed are the poor and woe to the rich, blessed are the hungry and woe are those who are full, blessed are the mournful and woe to the merry. We tend not to preach on Luke's set of beatitudes!

The Beatitudes follow a set pattern: "blessed are, theirs is." They are present tense and plural in form. In his being, Jesus brings the Kingdom of Heaven. The first words spoken by Jesus in Matthew, 4:17, are "Repent, for the kingdom of heaven is at hand." In Mark, his first words (1:15) "The time is fulfilled, the kingdom

of God is at hand, repent and believe the good news!" My hand is
attached to my body. If my hand has arrived, so has my entire body.
If the Kingdom is "at hand" it is very present, here and now, it has
arrived. Jesus believed he was bringing in the Kingdom of Heaven.
His followers entered this Kingdom by believing and lived in it by
following. In his being, Jesus brought in a new godly reign, a rule
of love rather than laws and a kingdom where everything is seen as
holy. In seminary we called this "realized eschatology," the time is
fulfilled, the Kingdom has come. Maybe not in full maturity, but
it has begun. Both the blessing and the Kingdom are present tense
and plural. This is not "pie in the sky by and by" and it is not "me
and my God." It is here and now and we enter it together.

There are social implications in the Beatitudes, as demonstrated by Luke's reversals in his woes. Matthew stays with the blessings
and focuses on their manifestations, revealing the presence of God
in our daily lives. Christianity is the earthiest of all world religions,
most concerned with people's welfare here and now. We build hos-
pitals and schools as well as churches, feeding bellies, caring for
bodies and nourishing brains as we build the Kingdom. Blessed
are those who give themselves to the reign of God among us, for
they will see it rise before their faces! The blessings are plural and
the kingdom is present.

The word translated "blessed" is the richest, strongest, fullest
term available: *makarios*, it is the blessedness of the gods, holy joy,
divine delight, heaven's own happiness, ecstatic, unquenchable joy
and delight, happiness and contentedness. It is not just "more of
the same" as our normal human happiness, it is better in quality as
well as greater in quantity.

These are not standards we need to meet, it is a description of
who we already are: blessed are the humble, the hurting, the hungry, the pure, the peaceful, the persecuted, for they are and theirs
is and forever will be.

"Blessed are the poor in spirit, for theirs is the kingdom of
heaven." The poor in spirit are the humble, the ones who know they
are not the center of this or any universe. They are open to receiving

something new rather than closed in on their own self-contentedness.

"Blessed are those who mourn, for they will be comforted." Those who mourn have gotten in touch with their own humanity, the fact that we are all mortal, limited, finite beings. Knowing our mortality means we know our humanity, and the word "human" is related to "humus," the dark rich fertile soil from which new life springs forth.

"Blessed are the meek, for they will inherit the earth." In Aristotle's philosophy of the Golden Mean, he described this meekness as the perfect balance between aggressiveness and acquiescence, between being a steam roller and a welcome mat. It means to be angry: at the right time, for the right reason, in the right manner, with the right expression, toward the right end, etc. Anger that is perfectly righteous! If you've ever met someone with righteous anger, you gain a new perspective on what it means to be "meek!" In regard to the earth, I like to think of this as gentleness, minimizing our footprint upon this earth, remembering that it is God's planet and only entrusted to us.

"Blessed are those who hunger and thirst for righteousness, for they will be filled." Jesus is clearly in the line of the Old Testament prophets, with Micah and "doing justice, loving mercy and walking humbly," (Micah 6:8) and Amos' "let justice roll down like waters and righteousness like an ever+flowing stream" (Amos 5:24). The kingdom of heaven is very much of this realm, and our striving for righteousness and justice is critical to accomplishing God's will.

"Blessed are the merciful, for they will receive mercy." We've all heard of the Eastern religions' "yin and yang" and "karma" and the expression "what goes around, comes around." I like the prayer "May my words be gentle and tender, for tomorrow I may have to eat them." There is a tendency to get what we have given!

"Blessed are the pure in heart, for they will see God." Kierkegaard describes purity of heart as willing one thing, the greatest good. Certainly if we will the greater good for everyone, we will be able to see that good in others. I've used a Shaker greeting: "The

Christ in me greets the Christ in thee and draws us together in love." If I look for the good in others, I will surely find it.

"Blessed are the peacemakers, for they will be called children of God." Note: "peace*makers*" not "peace*keepers*." Making peace can be a messy business. Most churches are eager to provide acts of mercy; working for peace necessarily includes working for justice, and that can become political. Without justice, there can be no lasting peace, and the justice must be just for all parties. Yet a just and sustainable society is a modern description of the kingdom of heaven in secular terms.

"Blessed are those who are persecuted for righteousness' sake, for theirs is the kingdom of heaven." The hungry and the humble, the meek and the mortal, the pure and the peaceful, all who are living in and for the reign of God in human society run the risk of rejection and persecution. I remember a description of Christians as being "insanely happy, incredibly brave and always in trouble." That certainly describes the Christians of the first century! With the first beatitude, we repeat the "blessed are, theirs is" theme: plural and present!

"Blessed are you when people revile you and persecute you and utter all kinds of evil against you on my account. Rejoice and be glad, for your reward is great in heaven, for in the same way they persecuted the prophets who were before you." We need to maintain a sense of perspective. While the kingdom is very much here and now, it is also so much more than merely here and now. The kingdom is more than me and my predicament and more than my time and place. The church is established by God, the only divine institution. As such, it will endure beyond time and not even the gates of hell can prevail against it. I do not know what the church of the future will look like and I will not live to see it, but I am confident there will be one!

It might be helpful to write your own paraphrase of the beatitudes, using common language.

*Blessed are those who are open, for they are able to receive.*

*Blessed are those who are empty, for they may be filled.*

*Blessed are those who walk gently upon the earth, for they will have an earth to walk upon!*

*Blessed are the honest, for they can handle reality.*

*Blessed are those who know their weaknesses as well as their strengths, for they will live balanced lives.*

*Blessed are the passionate, for their lives will be vital and meaningful.*

*Blessed are the compassionate, they know others by heart.*

*Blessed are the focused; seeing the target, they will be able to hit it.*

*Blessed are those who look for the best in others, they will see God ever before them. Blessed are all who make peace and seek justice, they are the building blocks of Heaven on earth!*

*Blessed are you when people abuse you, disrespect you, lie about you. Rejoice and be glad! That is just how Jesus was treated.*

We are the salt of the earth and the light of the world. Saltiness describes the very essence of salt. Of all our seasonings, salt is the only one that increases the intensity of the other seasonings. Pepper, lemon, sage, etc. all add their own distinct flavor. Salt increases the taste of the others. We cannot live without salt, yet salt, all by itself is bitter and overpowering.

We don't see the light itself, but by the light we see all else. Shining a light into our eyes is blinding; showing a light before our eyes is revealing. Light spreads, salt sprinkles, both adding to their surroundings without drawing attention to themselves, transforming their environments by giving themselves fully to it.

We let our light shine, let our salt flavor, that others may see the goodness and taste the fullness of a life lived in God, and join us in following the True and Living Way.

The church of the 21st century may be more like that of the 1st than that of the 20th. All the leaders of that 1st century church died off, their whole world fell apart before them. They were an oppressed and sometimes persecuted minority. Yet they found the good news, wrote the Gospel, practiced what they preached, gave their witness, and found a way not just to survive but to thrive, approximately doubling every decade through that tumultuous century. We can survive and thrive also!

Wherever we go, the bliss of heaven goes with us. Whatever we do, we do for God's glory. Whatever we say, we proclaim the Good News!

## A CALL TO REFLECTION

What is your first impression of the Beatitudes? Which one is your favorite? What questions do they raise for you?

## A CALL TO CONVERSATION

What does it mean to be "blessed"?

What is your impression of Christians being "incredibly brave, insanely happy and always in trouble"?

The author stresses that the Beatitudes are plural and present, "blessed are; theirs is." How is your congregation serving as an example of a blessed community?

## A CALL TO ACTION

How do you live out these Beatitudes? Being meek and merciful, pure in heart and peacemakers, hungering and thirsting for righteousness?

When have you felt persecuted for your faith? How have you suffered?

# A CALL TO PRAYER

Thank you, God, for your many blessings in our lives, and for life itself. Thank you for making us to be blessings for others. May we be so aware of your presence and guidance in our lives that hearing and heeding your will becomes second nature for us. For Jesus' sake. Amen.

# CHAPTER 3

# ABOLISH OR FULFILL?

Matthew 5:17-37

Let's be honest: we all have our favorite scripture passages, and we all have those passages we would prefer to forget. The first canon of scripture was by Marcion in the mid-2nd century. He included some of Luke and selections from Paul's letters and left out everything else, the rest of the New Testament and all of the Old. The early church nearly left out the Book of Revelation and came close to including the Shepherd of Hermes. Martin Luther wanted to omit Revelation and "the right straw epistle" of James. When Cyril and Methodius converted the warring Serbs in the 4th century, they chose not to translate Joshua and Judges with their tales of conquest, razing and pillaging. The Serbs were violent enough without being encouraged to destroy cities and slaughter populations for the glory of God.

I remember sitting with a fellow pastor over lunch. He shared his dilemma, struggling with the scriptures as his denomination struggled with what to do with LGBTQ members and pastors. I laughed.

"You do realize that we are sitting here eating pizza with sausage, an abomination, mixed with cheese, another abomination, wearing blended fabric, a third abomination, and instead of worrying about all these abominations we are casually participating in, you worry about one that in no way applies to either of us."

He quickly changed the subject.

We all have our favorite passages, and our least favorite. We have a way to interpret. I say that I read the Old Testament from the perspective of the New Testament because I am a Christian, not a Jew. I know I read the Hebrew scriptures differently. This is not to dishonor either tradition, but to recognize the difference. I read the epistles from the perspective of the gospels because my faith is in Christ, not in Paul. I read the narrative of the gospel from the perspective of the dialogue. This is why some Bibles have the words of Christ in red.

Jesus says, "I come, not to abolish, but to fulfill." It seems hard to tell the difference. In either case, they are ended. Fulfilling the law means completing it, accomplishing it, perfecting it, thus ending it. After saying this, Jesus gives six examples, "You have heard it said, but I say unto you … " Do not murder becomes do not be angry, do not commit adultery becomes do not lust. Laws regarding divorce, oaths, revenge and loving are at least reinterpreted if not done away with.

In a sense, Jesus is using the second of Stephen Covey's *Seven Habits of Highly Effective People*: "Begin with the end in mind." Remembering the point and purpose of the law, the spirit and not just the text.

Choosing to obey is a conscious decision. We live in the midst of widespread lawlessness. Corporations ignore commonly accepted accounting principles, industry standards and environmental impact for the sake of the bottom line. Do we always come to a full and complete stop at the intersection or do we slow down and roll through? How many cars go through an intersection after the light has turned red? I've counted as many as six! How many times, and by what speed, do we exceed the posted speed limit? All of these seemingly minor daily choices decide if we are law abiding or lawless.

The Jews had 613 laws to observe and obey. I lived for a while in a neighborhood near an Orthodox synagogue. Every Friday afternoon driveways would fill up with out of town cars as family arrived for the Sabbath observance. Driving on the Sabbath was forbidden and walking was restricted. I attended a class in seminary led by a rabbi. For our final session, he invited us to his synagogue for a tour and a meal. When the entrée was presented we knew immediately he was Reformed; he served a beef and cheese casserole. In strict kosher, meat and milk dishes must remain totally separated, in preparation and in serving. One of my New Testament professors spent some time in Israel and explained that the elevators stopped on every odd numbered floor. On the Sabbath, he could get out on the 5th floor and walk down to his apartment on the 4th, but he could not get out on the 3rd and walk up a flight — too much work!

Jesus says "The Sabbath was made for man and not man for the Sabbath." Paul writes in Romans 14 that some may honor one day over another and others observe all days the same, some account some food unclean and others consider all foods clean. Peter's vision is recorded in Acts 10, where God says "Don't call anything I have made unclean!"

The law on writing goes into great detail, regarding which hand is used, what liquid is used, what language is used or what is written upon, if two letters can be read together, it is a sin. Different examples of unlawful writing are described. Only if the writing is not permanent might it not be unlawful. This is only one of the 613 laws; there are 612 to go!

Of course, we could keep all 613 and still be a grouch. Keeping track of them all might in itself make us a grouch. Jesus' one law is the law of love: love God, love your neighbor, love yourself, love one another. We can't love and be a grouch!

Marcus Borg's *Conflict, Holiness and Politics in the Teachings of Jesus* explains that Jesus and the Pharisees agreed on the call to and the importance of holiness. They disagreed on what was holiness. The Pharisees held that purity was holiness, and so separated themselves from others. Jesus believed compassion was holiness, and therefore went out to and welcomed all.

When Jesus says, "You have heard it said, but I say," he raises the bar; he calls us to a higher code, a greater standard. Jesus says intention counts as much as action, that what goes on inwardly is as important as what goes on outwardly. He calls us to be authentic, to be true to ourselves. We've heard the expression, "Your actions speak so loud I cannot hear your words." How we behave is more important than, and a truer statement of, what we believe. Jesus challenges us to end the law, not by abolishing it but by accomplishing it, even in our hearts.

In the Kevin Costner movie, *Robin Hood: Prince of Thieves,* there is a line from Morgan Freeman's character, Azeem the Magnificent, "There are no perfect men in this world, only perfect intentions." No perfect actions, only perfect intentions. I doubt it. I doubt that I have ever had perfect intentions. Even in obeying the speed limit. I see myself as a patriotic American and law abiding citizen and a good role model. I also don't want to get caught! If I have mixed intentions in deciding how fast to drive, I have mixed intentions in everything.

Jesus calls us to resonance, to allow God to sound through us. "Let your 'Yes' be yes and your 'No' be no." As questions of obedience reveal the complexity of our will, the Law reveals the clarity of God's will. "Will" means the longing, yearning, desiring of God. When I think of "law," I think of something cold, uncaring, implacable. When I think of the yearning and desiring of God, I think of something warm, soft, loving and living. Let the law live, let it be written not on tablets of stone but the tablets of our hearts.

Jesus does not dispense with obedience, rather he invites it to be our loving response to God's loving desire for us, offering a new life, new way, new world, where our daily lives bear true obedience even as a tree bears good fruit. Jesus invites us to resonance, where our lives reverberate with the yearning of God, where intention and action are in sync, where will and witness are one, where the inner and the outer match.

Jesus also invites us to reverence, to fulfilling the law and the prophets, to respecting the law and the gospel, to see the law of God as the love of God. Reverence means great respect, honor, even affection. We are called to revere our brother and sister, our accuser and guard, the stranger and our spouse. Reverence for all life.

Will Rogers said, "There's no such thing as strangers, only friends I haven't met yet." Martin Buber wrote about having "I and

Thou" relationships rather than "I and it" where we live in honor, respect, affection, reverence, with the world.

Resonance between our inner and outer world, between intention and action, and reverence with the other, all the others, thus fulfilling the will, the longing and desiring of God for us and for all God's creation.

Ralph Waldo Emerson advised, "Watch your thoughts for they become words, watch your words for they become actions, watch your actions, for they become habits, watch your habits for they become character, watch your character, for it becomes your destiny."

Watch: words, actions, thoughts, character, habits equal "watch." As Psalm 141:3 prays, "Set a watch, O Lord, before my mouth, a door before my lips."

We have heard the Hindu greeting, "Namaste," literally meaning "I bow to you." It means to show respect and honor, to reflect reverence and resonance. "The best that is in me, welcomes and affirms the best that is in you." As the Shaker greeting says, "The Christ in me greets the Christ in thee and draws us together in love." Certainly this fulfills the law and the prophets!

# A CALL TO REFLECTION

How has the call to purity and the call to compassion worked themselves out in your life?

What do you think of the concept of "perfect intentions"?

# A CALL TO CONVERSATION

Jesus seems to consistently raise the bar, "you have heard it said, but I say to you ... " What do you think is his intent in doing this?

How do you understand Martin Buber's contrast between "I-Thou" relationships and "I — it" relationships?

How may we have called "unclean" what God has made "clean"?

## A CALL TO ACTION

Look at the relationships of your daily life. How can you emphasize them as "I — Thou" relationships rather than "I — it"?

Offer a silent blessing for each person before beginning a conversation with them. See how this affects the conversation and the relationship.

## A CALL TO PRAYER

God, you are that which is wholly different, wholly other, and Holy. And in your holiness, you are love. May I be a reflection of your love for all your children. May I see your love reflected in them. For Jesus' sake. Amen.

# Chapter 4

# Revolutionary Jesus

## Matthew 5:38-48

There is much talk from every sector about the church in politics. Politicians at least give lip service to their faith, especially during election cycles. Many who opt out of the church, find the church to be too political, too judgmental, too self-righteous, too hypocritical, too anti-LGBTQ, and too irrelevant for where they are in their daily lives. Other say the church should not get involved in political issues at all, maybe intoning James 1:27, "keeping one's self pure in the world."

I understand politics as any process of group decision making. A discussion and vote during a church board meeting is a political process. Deciding if the new church kitchen cabinets should be stained natural or painted white is a political process. Being involved in politics is inevitable; any human organization has politics as a part of its ongoing process. There may be good politics and poor politics, but "no politics" is not an option.

Our involvement in politics in the public sector is equally divisive, with Christians both pro-life and pro-choice, both supporting and opposing equal marital rights, and both supporting and opposing immigrant rights. This political involvement is also a natural part of our Christian faith; we are founded upon political involvement. Being involved in issues of social justice and the public good is part of our Christian DNA; the question is not if we will be involved, but how.

I think of my own United Church of Christ, in part founded by congregational separatists from England who opposed government support of religion and Puritans and Pilgrims who equated church membership with community citizenship. John Adams,

Paul Revere and Ben Franklin were all baptized at the Old South Congregational Church, where the original Boston Tea Party was organized and the lights were given to begin Paul Revere's ride. When the British occupied Philadelphia and confiscated bells to smelt into cannon balls, Zion Reformed Church in Philadelphia hid the Liberty Bell beneath the floor boards in their sanctuary; it exists today because of our church's historic involvement in political affairs. We stood up for the rights of the freed slaves on the *Amistad* slave ship and took Andrew Jackson to court over his reneging on our treaties with the Native Americans. John Brown wanted to become a Congregationalist pastor, but feared he could not take the rigors of ministry, so became a militant abolitionist instead. In more recent times, we defended public access to the airwaves by religious organizations, shut down our national synod early so we could march with Cesar Chavez and the Migrant Farm Workers, pushed for the Americans with Disabilities Act, ordained the first openly gay pastor and pushed for equal marital rights. For the United Church of Christ being politically involved is part of our DNA.

We can push Christian political involvement all the way back to the New Testament and to Christ himself. He was executed by crucifixion, a state sanctioned penalty for a crime against the state. The charge over his head was "Jesus of Nazareth, King of the Jews," not "savior" or "messiah," but "king," a political title. In the Lord's Prayer we are taught to pray for the coming of the Kingdom of God. Robert Cornwall entitled his book on the Lord's Prayer, *Ultimate Allegiance: The Subversive Nature of the Lord's Prayer.* In Jesus' teachings we learn that this kingdom is where the poor become rich, the empty filled, the hunger fed, the oppressed set free and the broken made whole. In the beginning of Luke's gospel various titles are ascribed to Jesus: "prince of peace," "son of God," "savior," and "Lord." All these are titles claimed by Augustus, emperor of Rome. Luke gives to Jesus the titles claimed by the supreme political leader of the most powerful empire then in existence. It seems that being politically involved is part of the very fabric of being Christian!

I believe the question is not "Is the church involved in politics?" or "Should the church be involved in politics?" but "How is the church involved in politics? How are we called to act out our faith within a political system?" I read both encouragement to be involved and instruction on how to be involved in the Sermon on the Mount.

Jesus tells us to turn the other cheek, to give cloak as well as coat and to go the extra mile. Within the context of first century Judah, what does this mean?

For both Roman and Jew, society in the first century was very hierarchical and strongly segmented; various sectors of society had no dealings with each other. This was especially true at meal times, yet throughout all the gospels Jesus is noted for practicing open table fellowship toward all: publican and Pharisee, sinner and disciple, men and women. Jesus preached and lived a radical new way.

In Matthew 5:39, we are told, if struck on one cheek to turn the other cheek. In the highly stratified society of the first century, striking with the back of the left hand was a clear insult. In many societies the left hand is used to insult others. If I strike you with the back of my left hand, I am adding insult to injury. I am demonstrating that I am your superior in every way. If you do as Jesus recommends and offer the other cheek, there is no way I can strike it with the back of my left hand. I might still strike it, but in striking you with my right hand instead of my left, I am demonstrating your equal status to mine. This is not playing the welcome mat, this is advocating active, non-violent resistance.

If you are my creditor and demand my outer garment as security and I give you my inner garment as well, I stand before you naked. This is an act of shame, but in the cultural setting of the first century, the shame is not on the one who is naked but rather on the one who sees another's nakedness — the creditor. Giving you my cloak as well as my coat is a way for me to bring shame on you and shame on an economic system that oppresses the poor.

Roman auxiliaries were permitted to force Jewish civilians to carry their backpacks the distance of one Roman mile; the civilian could be arrested or abused for refusing. The soldier could not compel a second mile, and could be punished if they did so. In Jesus' example, the first mile the soldier relaxes while you sweat carrying his heavy load. In the second mile, the soldier begs and pleads for you to please give him back his pack, lest he be punished.

In Matthew 5:44, Jesus summarizes how we are to act in the public sector by telling us to love our enemies and pray for our persecutors. Jesus was wise and observant enough to realize open rebellion to oppression would always fail. He also knew that ignoring the systemic oppression or passively accepting it was equally misguided. There needed to be a third way, a third choice. Jesus chose a path other than responding with violence to violence and other than passively accepting that violence, a way that would demonstrate the absurdity of the violence and demonstrate the viability of the third way.

All of these examples demonstrate the role reversal so common in Jesus' parables and other teachings. All of them demonstrate very real, practical ways for an oppressed majority to exert their worth through non-violent, active resistance. In *Jesus and Nonviolence: A Third Way*, Walter Wink makes a strong case for Jesus' use of active, non-violent resistance. The "first way" is the myth of redemptive violence. The "second way" is choosing the equally misguided passive response to the violence. The "third way" is the way of active, non-violent resistance. It is an argument Leo Tolstoy makes in *The Kingdom of God is Within You*.

To take two analogies from modern film, Jesus is like Neo in *Matrix*. Toward the end of the film, Neo realizes he is experiencing a projection in a computer matrix and he actually sees the code that supports the matrix. He sees a new reality, freeing him up from that once hidden code, and he moves beyond the game. Neo had been offered two pills by Morpheus. Jesus would see three pills: violent resistance, passivity and the third way of non-violent yet vigilant resistance. Another movie would be Matthew Broderick's *Wargames*, where Broderick is a computer genius who hacks a Defense Department computer that does not realize Broderick is only playing a game. The computer is setting up an actual nuclear war. After playing through countless scenarios, the computer realizes "The only way to win is not to play the game." Likewise, Jesus sees that the only way for the unarmed, disempowered, impoverished masses to win is to not play the game: not to attempt violence nor to passively acquiesce, to affirm one's dignity, to use humor to shame and ridicule those abusing their power and to consistently respond with non-violent resistance.

Inspired by the example of Jesus' life and his teachings in the Sermon on the Mount, Mahatma Gandhi led his fellow Indians in "resistance to evil by peaceful means" to attain their national independence. Martin Luther King, Jr. used the same "soul force" to attain the civil rights victories of the 1960's. Nelson Mandela converted from the violence of his early years to the same active non-violent resistance to end apartheid in South Africa. In each case, non-violent means were successfully used to achieve social transformation.

The example of the early church offers further evidence of the effectiveness of active non-violent resistance. Jesus was executed for the crime of rebellion against the state, claiming to be king. His followers were outlawed, ridiculed, sometimes persecuted. Yet the church grew each decade until, in 313 C.E. the church was legally sanctioned and by 325 C.E. the church became the official religion of the Roman Empire, effectively conquering the empire using only the "soul force" of Martin Luther King, Jr., the resistance by peaceful means, the power of love. The church becoming the official religion of the empire did carry its own complications, but the point remains that, using only non-violent means, the followers of this Jesus triumphed over the empire that executed him.

In every instance, when active non-violent resistance has been consistently applied and followed, it has triumphed over the abuse of power.

In the Sermon on the Mount, Jesus makes it clear that we are to welcome everyone, greet everyone, love everyone. In so doing, we attain the perfection that is divine. The word translated "perfect" in

Matthew 5:48, also means to be complete, finished, made whole, fulfilled. This is Jesus' vision of the kingdom on earth: a place where all people find their fulfillment.

"A place where all people find fulfillment" describes the Kingdom of God, describes Jesus' promise to his followers and describes the role of the church in modern day politics. It is a way and a world imagined by Martin Luther King Jr., as quoted by Walter Wink:

> "To our most bitter opponents we say: We shall match your capacity to inflict suffering by our capacity to endure suffering. We shall meet your physical force with soul force. Do to us what you will, and we shall continue to love you. We cannot in all good conscience obey your unjust laws, because noncooperation with evil is as much a moral obligation as is cooperation with good. Throw us in jail, and we shall still love you. Bomb our homes and threaten our children, and we shall still love you. Send your hooded perpetrators of violence into our communities at the midnight hour and beat us and leave us half dead, and we shall still love you. But be ye assured that we will wear you down by our capacity to suffer. One day we shall win freedom, but not only for ourselves. We shall so appeal to your heart and conscience that we shall win you in the process, and our victory will be a double victory."

This is our proper political path, in faith and in freedom. It is a path of active non-violent resistance, a path of love in action, a path whose effectiveness is demonstrated in our time by Gandhi and King and Mandela, a path proven by the generations of Christians who founded our faith.

## A CALL TO REFLCTION

"The Kingdom of God is a place where all people find fulfillment." If this is so, where does it exist? How does this describe your local church?

## A CALL TO CONVERSATION

What is your reaction to "turning the other cheek," "walking the second mile," and giving up cloak as well as coat, as acts of passive resistance to an oppressive regime?

What is your reaction to seeing Jesus as a political figure?

## A CALL TO ACTION

How can we model another way of life in our lives, a way where all are welcome, accepted, and find fulfillment? What is preventing us?

## A CALL TO PRAYER

God, your words are challenging as they are comforting. We seek the comfort and avoid the challenge. Give us the courage to act in ways consistent with your call in our lives, consistent with your promised kingdom. We pray for Jesus' sake. Amen.

# CHAPTER 5

## SUBVERSIVE PIETY

### Matthew 6:1-8, 16-18

Sally was a cute little girl: blond pony tail and blue eyes, a bit of a tomboy and a real love for "My Little Pony." She had every model and all the accessories. For her birthday, her parents decided to rent a pony — rent, not buy. She was ecstatic.

"Is it real? Is it real?" she sang as she danced in place.

"Yes, Sally, it's real."

"But is it really real?" she demanded.

What is real, and what is really real?

The closing scene in the movie *Matrix* has Neo going head to head against Mr. Smith in a great and final battle. The climax comes when Neo looks at Mr. Smith and sees the computer program code that creates the image of Mr. Smith. Seeing the code puts Neo in charge, and he wins the day. Neo saw what was really real.

Neo might be a Christ figure. Jesus sees all that is, and sees the God who is before, beneath and beyond all that is. God is that code which creates, as God said to Moses, "I am what causes to be."

Whatever else he was, Jesus was a spiritual prodigy, like Confucius, Buddha, Mohammed. He envisioned a different world: beginning his ministry with "The time is fulfilled, the Kingdom of God is at hand, repent and believe the good news!" He saw himself introducing and embodying a new world, warning Pilate, "My kingdom is not of this world." A new way of living and being, a new way of seeing; in John's Gospel he is "the true and living way." Jesus is a spiritual revolutionary and the Sermon on the Mount is his manifesto. The hungry are fed, the empty filled, the poor made rich, the last become first, the broken made whole, the wounded healed. Jesus is intent on making this Kingdom of God, Kingdom of Heaven, a kingdom of righteousness and peace, of joy and power, a new reality on earth.

We sometimes miss or forget the radicalness of the Gospel.

Jesus tells us to turn the other cheek, to offer a cloak as well as coat, to walk a second mile. Now we realize that he is really speaking of a third way. He sees the Roman occupation, the military suppression, the oppression of wealthy Jews over the peasant class, the subjugation of the masses achieved by the sacrificial system imposed by the high priests. He also knows violence to violence only creates more violence. Violent resistance is not the answer. Neither is passive compliance. The system is a failed system; passivity merely continues the evil.

The third way is active, non-violent resistance: using humor to point out the absurdity of a power structure gone bad, making fun of its futility and failure, and to affirm the dignity and worth of each individual: peasant and priest, fisherman, carpenter and centurion. The third way is not to play the game, but to join Jesus in his movement to create a new world, new life, new kingdom. In a closed, segmented society peopled with untouchables, Jesus welcomes one and all to come and follow, to feast at his banqueting table, to join him on the way. It is a radical approach and a radical offering, striking at the root of the world as it was.

This Way is no less radical in our day. We do not have an occupying army or a priestly class, but we are not a classless society or one that promotes upward mobility. The income of our top one percent is up nearly 150%, while that of the 99 is stagnant. Sometime in 2016, the top 1% will control over half of the world's total income, leaving less than half for the 99. We do have inequalities in our system.

In terms of religion, the fastest growing group in America is the "nones," "none of the above" or "no religion." Agnostics and atheists are in vogue. We live in a very secular society; any religious influence is dwindling. We are also a very consumerist, materialist society. After 9/11, President Bush's response was to encourage us to express our patriotism by going out and buying something. Our materialism pervades our culture. We tend to live as if the material world is all there is, our sole purpose is to consume as much as we can and it is all about us. What did Madonna say? "I'm a material girl living in a material world and the boy with the cold hard cash is Mr. Right." We catch ourselves living as if the materialism of this world is enough and there is no spiritual, as if it all were show without substance, noise without nuance, material without meaning.

Jesus warns us about practicing our piety. Note Jesus says "when," not "if." In a world that believes only in materialism, consumerism and individualism, practicing piety is a radical act, a subversive act. Piety is believing there is more than a merely material world, that life is sacred and not secular, profound and not profane, that everything is holy now, that spiritual reality is very much a part of our existence. Piety is devotion to the divine. Piety is behaving as if we believe.

In this reading, three practices are listed: giving, praying and fasting. Others typically include self-examination, scripture reading, acts of service. In his modern classic, *Celebration of Discipline*, Quaker author Richard Foster identifies twelve practices. His son, Nathan Foster, has shared quite personally of his struggle and response to his father's writing in his own *The Making of an Ordinary Saint*. My point is the radical nature of practicing any piety. Any authentic piety will strike at the core of our being.

When we give, we give because the need is real, because the other person matters as much as we do; because it is not all about us, we are a family, we are all part of the whole. The needs of others are as real as our needs, and what we have, we have together. We do what is right because it is right and not because it is popular or will get us noticed. As Jesus says in 5:42, "Give to anyone who asks; don't refuse anyone." Because we are all one and what we have, we have together. Is that radical enough?

When we pray, we don't need loud noises or lots of words. We know that every breath is a prayer, every word is worship, every thought a petition, every act a witness, every step a sign. As Brother Lawrence of the Resurrection said, "I would not so much as pick up a piece of straw from the ground but for the love of God." As Paul wrote, "Rejoice always, pray constantly, give thanks in all circumstances, for this is God's will for us in Jesus Christ" (1 Thessalonians 5:16-18).

Fasting may be the most radical practice of all. Fasting demonstrates that there is more than a merely material world and we are meant for more than simply consuming. There is more to the world and there is more to us. Jesus says of our material world, "don't lay up for yourselves treasures that rust, corrode, deteriorate or decay; rather, do lay up treasures" — yes, gaining treasures is a good thing, we just want to accumulate the right ones, the ones that don't rust, corrode or decay, that can't be stolen.

None of this is out of charity. Charity is sharing our scraps, letting others have the crumbs we no longer want. Justice is welcoming them to the table with us, recognizing our essential equality and ultimate unity. In the pious acts of the Kingdom of God, the poor are made rich, the broken made whole, the empty are filled and the last become first. This is divine justice, not human charity.

The New Testament is intentionally communal; in Acts "they held all things in common." In a trick of linguistics, if we changing the "i" to "we" changes "illness" to "wellness"! With Pope Francis we hear the warning: Society is secular, we believe all is sacred. Society is individualistic, we are a community and family. Society is consumerist, we say it's what we give, not get, about sharing not hoarding. Greed is based on scarcity; we believe in Abundance, not anxiety. Society is materialist; we are spiritual. When we behave as we believe, our piety is subversive, undermining current trends & establishing a new way.

Jesus reminds us to remember our reality, to behave as we believe. His harshest words in all scripture are for the hypocrites, the play-actors, those who only pretend to believe. Jesus' words to these pretenders are sharp, "They have received their reward," "They've got all they are going to get." Like the senior pastor sharing with the new intern: "What the people really want is for you just to be real, be genuine, be sincere, authentic. If you can fake that, you've got it made."

Practicing this piety is subversive. It is saying to this world that there is more and that materialism and consumerism and individualism is not the answer. There is a spiritual reality; we are all connected. Practicing this piety undermines the way of this world and establishes the True and Living Way. Jesus challenges us to be real in our faith, to behave as if we believe. This level of openness brings with it a certain vulnerability. If we are authentic and open, then we are open to being hurt and exposed. Authenticity takes courage; being real means being brave.

I was serving Joyce Chapel United Methodist Church while in seminary. Methodist churches always have communion rails around the chancel, so that we can kneel when we take Communion. One Sunday I had taken the rails down to open up the area around the altar. One of our members was visibly distraught. "I feel naked," she said. I thought about that. I think we do stand naked before God, that is the only way we can stand before the Divine. God already knows all my secrets. God knows the stuff I would never share. God knows I'm overweight, near-sighted, short tempered; God knows I'm an introvert and really don't want to share.

God already knows. "The God who sees in secret." If God knows, I might as well admit it. I may as well be real. In *The Velveteen Rabbit* there is a scene with the Rabbit and the Skin Horse about "being real." Being real is about being open to love, open to being loved especially. Being loved and loving is being real and really real!

Practicing our piety is subversive, not just because it undermines the way of this world and establishes the True and Living Way, but because it exposes our personal illusions, private imaginations, secret conceits. Practicing my piety means that I know that God knows all my faults and failures, and uses them like flaws in a diamond, to radiate and shine God's glory even through me.

## A CALL TO REFLECTION

Do we see the radical nature of living out our piety? How are we being counter-cultural as an expression of our understanding of God?

How is the world view of our culture different from the world view of the gospel?

## A CALL TO CONVERSATION

Where in our lives are we challenged to be authentic, to be "really real"?

When was a time you felt naked before God?

## A CALL TO ACTION

Jesus gives instructions for when we give, pray and fast. How big a role are the spiritual disciplines in our lives? How can we strengthen them?

## A CALL TO PRAYER

You know us, God; even in our deepest prayers, we tend to focus more on ourselves than on you. May we lose ourselves in our prayers. May we learn the truth of "less of me, more of Thee." Pray your prayer in us and through us, that we may become living prayers. For Jesus' sake. Amen.

# CHAPTER 6

# PLEDGING ALLEGIANCE

Matthew 6:9-15

As school children we learn the Pledge of Allegiance, reciting it every morning. It is so familiar that we can repeat it without thinking about it. The Lord's Prayer is our Christian "pledge of allegiance." It is a verbal testimony of our faith and commitment, words we learned when children, and so familiar that we can repeat it without thinking.

There is probably no more familiar piece of scripture in any religion than The Lord's Prayer. Every adult Christian, of any denomination or tradition, knows it. It is better known than any of the creeds or any other passage, with the possible exception of the Twenty-third Psalm. Many of other faiths are familiar with it. Even atheists in the West would recognize it. Further, it is the one thing Jesus' disciples asked him to teach them. Jesus performed miracles, fed thousands, gave sight to the blind, walked on water and raised the dead. The disciples did not ask to be able to do any of those. Instead, they asked "Lord, teach us to pray."

This prayer is a bold, radical statement of faith; praying it is a subversive act. We grow too familiar with the words, we say them without thinking them, without allowing them to soak into our souls. They call for the coming of another culture, another kingdom. Listen to them!

The Lord's Prayer consists of seven petitions. The first three focus on God, the last four focus on us, just as the first four of the Ten Commandments focus on God and the last six on us. There is a balance, but both begin with the divine. The true focus is on God, not on us. Our society is extremely self-absorbed, self-obsessed. The Lord's Prayer begins and ends with the divine.

"Our." The very first word is a challenge to our culture. The Lord's Prayer is a communal prayer, a corporate act. There is no "I, Me, Mine" in it. It is entirely and exclusively plural: "our Father," "give us," "forgive us," lead us," "deliver us." There is no "I," only "us." When we get caught up in our opinions and emotions, we best remember. Our culture tells us "have it your way," "if you want it, you need it," our wants becoming needs and our desires becoming necessities. I can have it all now, and pay for it for the rest of my life. The Lord's Prayer is not about me; it is about us.

"Our Father." "Father." All religions understand a transcendent God, a God who is the Holy Other, above and beyond. The mystics of all religions experience a God who is immanent, a God with whom we may be intimate, though most would hesitate to be too familiar with the holy. The Hebrew Scriptures do speak of God as the Father of Israel. But this is not what Jesus describes; he would not call God "father" as I call my dad "father" or as my children might refer to me. Jesus spoke of "Abba," like an infant's babbling sound for this big, strong, awesome, gentle, loving presence. "Dada" or "Papa."

It is one month old Declan or four month old Evan or 2 ½ year old Ryker. Even Alex at 6 has outgrown the magical mystical intimate wonder of the unconditional trust and abiding confidence of this relationship. Our God is our Abba, our Amma, our strong, gentle, abiding Presence.

"In Heaven." Heaven is not a time or a place, not a planet orbiting some distant star, not a place people go when they die. Heaven is a living relationship with a loving God, heaven is being in the Divine Presence. Jesus defines eternal life, "Eternal life is to know you, the one true God, and Jesus Christ whom you have sent" (John 17:3). Heaven is being in this living, loving relationship with divinity itself. Heaven is here and now, if we would have it so. Experiencing this relationship causes us to realize that everything is holy now, that the sacred surrounds us, the eternal envelopes us, the holy is in the here and now.

"Your kingdom come, your will be done, on earth as in heaven." Here is the overthrow of the ordinary. Our country fought a revolutionary war to rid itself of a king, and here we pray for a new kingdom, the Kingdom of God. The reign of God is where the will of God is done, where the deeds Christ challenges us to do, are accomplished. The naked are clothed, the hungry are fed, the thirsty given drink, the homeless sheltered, the stranger welcomed, the imprisoned visited, the sick made well, where no one suffers lack. Is this the country where we live, or are we praying for another one, a better place, where the love of God is made manifest, where the glory of God is revealed, where the grace of God is shared with all?

We are praying for God's heaven to make itself known in our time and our place. Heaven on earth, here and now. God's will be done by president and governor and mayor, by senator and representative, and yes, by each and every citizen, by you and by me. "Not to us, O Lord, not ever to us, but to your name be glory and to your name be praise, for your steadfast love is great toward us and your faithfulness endures forever" (Psalm 115:1). This is truly revolutionary!

After these three petitions for God come the four for us.

"Give us this day our daily bread." "Us" and "our," we are all in this together. I am responsive to your needs as you are to mine and we are together. "Give us what we truly need today." As Jesus says elsewhere in the Sermon (Matthew 6:34) "Let the day's own trouble be sufficient for the day." When Israel was in the wilderness and God fed them with manna from heaven, they were to take only what they could eat that day. So we pray for the needs of this day alone.

Some commentaries remind us that we have spiritual needs as well as physical ones, that the bread may be "super substantiated." We need to feed the heart as well as the belly. We've all had occasion to stand before an open refrigerator unable to find what we are looking for. Maybe it's because we need to feed our spirits as well as our stomachs. It is as the hymn says, "all our gifts have come from Thee and of Thine own have we given Thee."

"Forgive us our debts as we have forgiven others." Forgiving our souls is as critical as feeding our stomachs. And again, it is all in the plural, "forgive us our debts as we have forgiven our debtors." This is the only petition that is made conditional. "If you forgive others, you will be forgiven; if you do not forgive, you will not be forgiven" (Matthew 6:14-15). In John, Jesus says, "What you bind on earth will be bound in heaven, what you loose on earth will be loosed in heaven. If you forgive the sins of any, they are forgiven; if you do not forgive, they are not forgiven."

No one is compelled to be a Christian. We can choose any faith or no faith. If we choose to be Christian, we must forgive, we must love. Love is not a request or a suggestion, but a commandment: love God, love neighbor, love one another, love our enemy, even love ourselves. If we choose to be Christian, we must forgive.

I worked for Mennonite Mutual Aid in Goshen, Indiana. A Mennonite couple drove from Goshen to Terre Haute to visit a convict in the state prison there. They need to, they were compelled, it was urgent that they see the man. He had kidnapped, abused, tortured and murdered their daughter, and it was essential to them that he knew they had forgiven him. They could not go another day without making sure he knew he was forgiven. I am not saying forgiving is easy; I am saying it is essential. If we are Christian, we must forgive. That certainly is a bold, radical, subversive statement, yet it is precisely what Christ compels!

"Lead us not into temptation." No, I can find that all by myself. I even know a shortcut! When I was a boy we were going on vacation to the beaches in Florida. The men of the church joked with their pastor, my father, "Be careful on those beaches! There will be a lot of young ladies in skimpy suits, a lot of temptation!" Dad joked right back, "It's only temptation if you resist!" I've used that line often in reference to chocolate. Let's face it: most of us need no help in finding temptation all by ourselves. God does not, would not, lead any of us into temptation.

The passage describes a testing time, a time for us to prove our mettle, a sifting of the chaff from the wheat and a smelting of the ore from the gold. We'd just as soon not go through hard times, and if we must, then we pray that God will accompany us.

"Deliver us from evil" or "the Evil one." There is chaos in the world, things unexpected do happen. We pray for the coming of God's kingdom and the doing of God's will, which would totally disrupt the world we live in. So we also pray for guidance and deliverance, that as we pursue the divine we may also find shelter in the storm.

"For thine is the kingdom and the power and the glory forever. Amen." This phrase is not in the text of Matthew or Luke, but soon attached by worshippers in the early church and part of the prayer in every Protestant tradition. Bringing us back to the beginning, focusing our attention again on the divine and not on ourselves. It is counter-cultural for people to live for the sake of someone or something else, and Christians live for the sake of Christ and for the coming of the kingdom of God.

When we pray this prayer, we change the world because we change ourselves.

Our Jewish friends are to pray three times a day. Our Muslim friends are to pray five times a day. Our cloistered Christians pray seven times a day. Buddhist monks will pray several hours each day. *The Didache* calls us to pray The Lord's Prayer three times daily.

My daughter-in-law is a dental hygienist who reminds me to brush my teeth for two minutes twice a day. So I pray The Lord's Prayer when I brush my teeth. Once through with the uppers and once through with the lowers. I pray the Jesus Prayer, "Lord Jesus Christ, Son of God, have mercy on me, a sinner," when I gargle. Once through with the right cheek, once through with the left cheek, once with the upper lip and once with the lower lip. Then I throw my head back and gargle, while I repeat mentally The Lord's Prayer again.

I don't share this so that you will think I'm some kind of great spiritual prayer warrior. We all know better than that. I share this as testimony to prayer as essential and to its efficacy. If I have to pray this much just to be at this level, imagine how bad of shape I'd be in without it! We need to pray!

## A CALL TO REFLECTION

Pray The Lord's Prayer silently, slowly, reflecting on each phrase and word. Breathe it into your body and listen to it speak to you. Let this prayer be Jesus, praying in, with, for and through you.

## A CALL TO CONVERSATION

Do you remember first praying The Lord's Prayer? What other prayers have you memorized? How has memorizing prayers or passages helped in your faith development?

## A CALL TO ACTION

Our Muslim friends find a way to pray five times each day. Each day for one week, follow the direction of *The Didache*: pray the Lord's prayer every morning, noon and night. Find a quiet place where, for ten minutes, you can remember and repeat the words and intentions of this prayer. How does this exercise change the rest of your day?

## A CALL TO PRAYER

God, who loves us more than mother or father, you are holy beyond our knowing or naming. May I do your will, may I be a sign of your presence and promise in this world, this day and every day. Give me what I need for this day. Forgive me and help me to forgive others. Lead me where you would have me go, deliver me from dangers only you can see. For it is all for your rule, your will, your glory, now and forever. Amen.

# CHAPTER 7

# FOCUS ON FAITH

### Matthew 6:19-34

Remember when gas prices were under two dollars? I remember gas wars in my college days and paying 24.9 cents per gallon! I remember black and white television shows and telephones hard wired to the wall. My dad is quite the classical music buff. If he sings in the shower, it is opera. I remember listening to vinyl recordings in monoraul sound, and the incredible rush when I first heard a recording in stereophonic sound. Different sound from different speakers! It was incredible.

We have two ears to help us better locate the source of any sound, two eyes to give us depth perception and target in on an image. There is a value in having two. Some of us try to multi-task: drive the car, talk on the cell phone, follow our GPS, eat a donut, drink coffee, change the radio, all at once. The problem with this is that studies indicate we do lose our concentration; our driving ability is impaired as if we were drunk. Jesus warns, "No one can serve two masters. Either he will hate the one and love the other, or he will be devoted to the one and despise the other." (Matthew 6:24) There are times we need a single focus.

In the movie *City Slickers*, Billy Crystal plays the part of a middle aged man trying to find a sense of purpose and fulfillment for his life. At a western dude ranch, he meets a cowhand named Curly, played by Jack Palance, who has found the secret: "One thing," Curly says, "find it, keep it, follow it." Yogi Berra said, "If you don't know where you're going, it doesn't matter how you get there." Curly would say, "Find your one path and stick to it."

In Jesus' day, some believed light entered the body through the eye. If the eye was clear, light brought life, health and vitality to the whole body. If the eye were clouded, the inner person would dwell in darkness. "The eye is the lamp of the body" (Matthew 6:22). We've heard the expressions of a good eye and an evil eye and understand what these colloquialisms mean. A clear eye is a good and generous eye; a cloudy eye is greedy and grudging.

In *Purity of Heart*, Soren Kierkegaard reflected on Matthew 5:8, "Blessed are the pure of heart, for they shall see God." Purity of heart is to will one thing, to live with a single focus. That "one thing" is to will the good for the other, to will what is best. Paul Tillich warns us that whatever is our ultimate concern, whatever it is that drives us and grounds us, is, for us, our God.

We can't serve two masters, two gods, two ultimate concerns. We can't serve God and Money. Please note that in the New International Version, "Money" is capitalized, making it clear that the worship of worldly wealth is idolatry. We cannot serve the divine cause and our own individual interests. We live in an incredibly materialistic world, a strongly consumerist culture. We are like the seagulls in *Finding Nemo*, screaming "Mine! Mine!" as we fight one another for a fresh catch. We are Gordon Gecko in *Wall Street*, lecturing that "Greed is good," while we make a living that says, "Greed is God!" We cannot serve these two masters.

Jesus reminds us what is lasting, what is eternal, what will support us in the storm. Not things, but people. It is about "we" not "me." Jesus invites us to be generous rather than greedy, share rather than hoard, to see what we can give rather than what we can get, where life touches life. There is our greatest treasure, our "one thing," and there will we find our heart. Jesus invites us to live in the "as if" of God, and in our living it, causing it to be so. As we work together for the common good and the glory of God, we discover our greatest treasure, our "one thing," and find our own fulfillment as a by-product.

In his classic *Making All Things New: An Invitation to the Spiritual Life*, Henri Nouwen reflects on Matthew 6:33, "Seek first God's rule and righteousness, and all these other things will be given you as well." Or as Bobbie McFerrin used to sing, "Don't worry, be happy." Worry never accomplished anything!

Nouwen describes our lives as filled yet unfulfilled, busy yet bored, hectic, hurried and scattered. We are pre-occupied, living beside ourselves or even in spite of ourselves, unfocused. We are about "all these other things" rather than "setting our hearts." We need to let go of the many and take hold of the One. We need to be present to ourselves, in our own lives. Our days may be like the storm of a hurricane, but even a hurricane has a calm center, the eye of the storm. We can find that calm center: God's reign, God's rule, God's righteousness, in our lives. Biblically, righteousness is about right relationships with one another, not keeping rules and regulations. God's righteousness is intimately personal. It is a glory beyond Solomon's and a wealth beyond this world.

## A CALL TO REFLECTION

What are some of the changes you have seen during your life? How have they improved your life? How have they challenged you?

Consider your personal priorities. Can you name the "one thing" in your life?

## A CALL TO CONVERSATION

When was a time that attempting to multi-task led to trouble or frustration? When have you attempted too much, and what were the consequences?

How has the conflict between culture and Christ played out in your life?

## A CALL TO ACTION

Find three things in your life that you can let go of, things that may have proven to be distractions to what you most value.

# A CALL TO PRAYER

May I seek your will for my life, God, and may I find it. In finding you, I find myself. Help me be present to you, God, that I may be present to myself. For Jesus' sake. Amen.

# CHAPTER 8

# KEEPING IT SIMPLE

## Matthew 7:1-20

I had an old vinyl live concert recording of Ike and Tina Turner, titled "What you hear is what you get!" I am reminded of the recording in reading this passage where Jesus talks about being judged as we judge others and treating others as we want to be treated. Taoists speak of yin and yang, Hindus have karma. Martin Luther King, Jr. said "The arc of history is long, but it bends toward justice." The Old Testament promises, "cast your bread upon the waters and it will come back to you." We've heard the expression "What goes around, comes around." Do we really think people get what they deserve? Do we treat others as we would like to be treated, or do we treat them as they have treated us? Do we hear this passage as a word of encouragement or a word of warning?

Is our treatment of others proactive or reactive, creative or contingent? Is it based on past behavior or is it a foundation for future behavior? If Jesus is a radical prophet of a bold new world, then, as his followers, our behavior should be based upon that promised future, as seeds planted along the way, rather than behavior based on how the world may have treated us. We are invited to be proactive and creative rather than reactive and contingent.

We are expressly forbidden to judge. Our self-examination and discernment is enough to keep us busy. We cannot know what another has experienced, what has gone in to making them who they are. We have not walked their path. We see only outer appearances, present consequences of past circumstances. The small round loaf of bread may have the appearance of a stone; the elongated fish or eel of Galilee may have the appearance of a snake. In Luke's Gospel, the egg may have the appearance of a resting scorpion. We see only outer appearances, not inner realities, not the inner essence of the person. We cannot judge.

We are here to love one another, not to judge one another. Remember, every time we point one finger at another, four of our fingers point back to us! I remember the "Five Fingers of Faithful Fellowship:" accept one another, welcome one another, encourage one another, pray for one another and, the opposable thumb connecting these four fingers, do it all non-judgmentally, do it all with love.

In a monastic community, one young monk had been caught stealing and an elder monk was called in to sit as judge. The elder monk refused at first, and then reluctantly agreed. First, he took a sack from the granary and hefted it over his shoulder. Seed from the sack spilled out behind him. When he arrived at the place for the trial, he set down the grain sack and said, "My own sin falls out behind me and I do not see it, and you would have me sit in judgment over another?"

Every religion, faith or wisdom tradition from around the world expresses the Rule of Reciprocity: don't do to others what you don't want done to yourself. East or West, Baha'i to Wiccan, religious or secular, all faith and wisdom traditions universally teach this rule. However, this is not quite the way Jesus teaches it.

If I were to sit and do nothing all day, I would satisfy the Rule of Reciprocity, of not doing to others what I don't want done to me. If I do nothing, I can do no harm. But this is not what Jesus says. He says "*Do* treat others as I *do* want to be treated." It is a positive, not a negative. "Not doing" will not suffice. I must do, I must act. I must treat others as I want to be treated, as my equals and in mutual relationship. As a "thou" rather than an "it." Passively not doing anything wrong will not satisfy Jesus' Golden Rule. I must actively do the positive. This is living and working so that the pledge of our allegiance in The Lord's Prayer may be satisfied: doing God's will on earth as in heaven, that God's reign may come among us, in and through the actions of our daily lives.

As John Wesley's motto declares, "Do all the good you can, by all the means you can, in all the ways you can, in all the places you can, at all the times you can, to all the people you can, as long as ever you can." Don't worry about what we can't do, but what we can do. In the name of God — do!

There is also the platinum rule, built upon the Golden Rule, yet recognizing the differences among us: "Treat other people as they most prefer to be treated." If someone prefers a back rub, don't scratch their back but rub it; if they most prefer a back scratch, scratch it, not rub it.

It is our deeds that count, not our words. As James 2:16 says, if we say to someone, "be warm and well fed" and do nothing about it, our words are empty and void. Our behavior demonstrates the truth of what we believe. One of our United Church of Christ slogans is "To believe is to care, to care is to do." In this sense, Christianity is a very personal and practical faith. I would say the unchurched today, especially the millennials, don't care about what we say we believe; they are only focused on how we actually behave. Our behavior demonstrates the truth of our beliefs! The suffering of any of us is a lessening of all of us. We are here not to tear down but to build up. "May my words today be tender and gentle, for tomorrow I may have to eat them."

Jesus' harshest words in all the gospels is toward the hypocrites, the play actors, those only pretending to be faithful. They are the hypocrites who are blind guides, whitewashed tombs, and who bother about another's speck while ignoring their own log. I have enough of my own sin, my own faults and flaws and shortcomings, that I need never worry about those of another. I am determined to know nothing but love.

## A CALL TO REFLECTION

Do we believe that people get what is coming to them, whether it be karma or the arc of history?

How can we manage our predilection to judge other people?

## A CALL TO CONVERSATION

When was a time that first impressions proved otherwise, that what we initially thought of a person proved to be mistaken?

What is the practical difference between "judging another" and being a "fruit inspector"? How can we be the latter without becoming the former?

## A CALL TO ACTION

Every day this week, make a point of doing something good for somebody else, perhaps without their knowing it and without their re-paying it. Perform random acts of kindness!

## A CALL TO PRAYER

God, you see the heart of the matter, you see the inner person and not just the outer appearance. Grant me your vision, that I may act with your intention. Help me to see as you see. For Jesus' sake. Amen.

# CHAPTER 9

# STANDING THE STORM

Matthew 7:21-29

I was hiking with my son Jason in the hills around Hollywood and we were talking about California earthquakes. Why was the ground so liable to shifting? It seemed to be solid bedrock, what caused it to be so weak? Jason reached his hand into the rocky cliff — yes, into. He grabbed a fistful of this seemingly solid rock and broke it off. Stretching his arm out before me, he squeezed the rock and it turned to powder in his grasp. I was dumbfounded. Did he have a great hidden strength?

"It's de-stressed granite, Dad. It is once-hardened rock that has been without outer stress for so long that it has lost its inner integrity. Now, whenever the stress of an earthquake hits, it just turns to sand."

One man built his house on rock, and one on sand.

Jesus, the radical prophet of a bold new age, urges us to have a firm, fruitful faith. We are challenged to hold on to a faith that is unshakable, that stands up to the storms of life. We are encouraged to live a faith that bears fruit, a faith that makes a practical difference in the lives of others. We are called to have a faith that is true, that sees a vision of that bold new age and tangible and visible in the present time.

It is not those who call Jesus "Lord," not those who perform spectacular stunts or attract large followings, who build monuments or movements or accumulate notable reputations, but simply those who do God's will, those who live it out in their daily lives. As Mother Theresa said, "Do small things with great love."

There are false prophets everywhere; every profession has its impostors. "Didn't we build massive cathedrals in your name, attract huge followings in your name, write bestselling books in your name?" Micah responds, "What does the Lord require, but to do justice, to love mercy, and to walk humbly with your God?" (Micah 6:8). It is not about being famous; it is about being faithful! True worship, authentic faith, real religion, is to care for and about one another, to care for the helpless, widows and orphans in their need, and keep one's self faithful even in a sometimes faith-less world (James 1:27).

Between being a United Methodist pastor and becoming a pastor in the United Church of Christ, I spent a decade in financial services: insurance and investments. I quickly discovered that my real product had not changed. As pastor and as advisor, my true product was really the trust relationship I established, whether with clients or parishioners. People wanted to know if they could trust me, if they could believe what I asked them to believe. A sense of personal integrity, authenticity, being "really real." As Shakespeare wrote, "To thine own self be true. And it must follow, as the night the day, that thou cans't not prove false to any [one]." If we are not honest with ourselves, we cannot be honest with another.

While we are not to judge others, we can be fruit inspectors, to know people by the fruit their lives bear, fruit that is good and fruit that endures. It is by the fruit of our lives that we prove our faith. It is not enough for us to work deeds of charity, to help people who are hurting, if we do nothing about the source of their distress. We become like the medic at the foot of a cliff where people are falling rather than the carpenter at the top of the cliff, building a fence to keep people from falling. Works of charity and mercy are a good thing, they help people who are hurting, but they do nothing to address systemic problems that cause the pain in the first place. A firm, fruitful faith requires that we address the systemic inequalities in our society that create pain and suffering and inhibit the full expression of human potential. Putting coins in a bucket of a worker displaced by global competition is not preparing that person a better future where they can be productive members of society. Again, the suffering of any of us lessens all of us. If we are serious about our pledge of allegiance, "thy kingdom come, thy will be done," then we must address social justice issues that allow full participation in our society and equal opportunities for all.

There is such a thing as a healthy tension. No tightrope walker wants a slack rope, but instead a rope that is pulled tight at both ends and strengthened by that stress. Even granite, used for the foundation of skyscrapers, loses its internal integrity if it goes too long without external stress.

A grandmother once comforted her granddaughter going through some difficult times. The grandmother filled three bowls with boiling water. In one bowl she put a piece of carrot, in the second an egg and in the third a tea bag. After several minutes, she said, "Sometimes we find ourselves in hot water. We can be the carrot, once crisp turned soft by our situation. We can be the egg, turned hard and tough on the inside. Or we can be the tea bag and give ourselves to changing the situation we are in."

Jesus makes it clear: it is not enough to hear these words or understand these words or agree with these words, we must act on them! I have read his closing parable on the house built on sand and the house built on rock and preached sermons on our lives being built on sand or on rock and missed the larger point. There is a storm coming! Whatever we have built in our lives, however we have built it, and wherever we have chosen to build it, there is a storm coming. Be prepared! Rock or sand, mountain or valley, there is a storm coming, be prepared!

## A CALL TO REFLECTION

How has stress been a positive factor in your life?

How do you work on being authentic?

How does the phrase, "a firm, fruitful faith" describe your faith?

## A CALL TO CONVERSATION

What has been the rock and the sand in your life?

What is a storm that you have survived?

## A CALL TO ACTION

Given that storm in life are inevitable, how can you prepare yourself for those upcoming storms?

## A CALL TO PRAYER

When the storms of life are raging, Lord, stand by me. Through the storm, through the night, through questions and doubts, may I always know your steadfast love and abiding faithfulness. See me through. For Jesus' sake. Amen.

# CHAPTER 10

# TRANSFORMATION: WHAT NEXT?

"When Jesus finished, the crowd was astounded at his teaching. He taught by his own authority, not as their teachers of the law."

The typical rabbinical teaching of the day was for the teacher, the rabbi, to ground their teaching in the writings of the Law or the Prophets, basing their teaching on what Moses said. In some instances, they might reference their teaching to the teaching of other well known and respected rabbis, like Gamaliel or Hillel said. Jesus did not teach as the other teachers did; he did not base his teachings on the teachings of other rabbis or on the scriptures every Jew had memorized as a child. Instead, he taught on his own authority.

Jesus is not just a wandering Galilean rabbi, not just another prophet in the Old Testament tradition, not just a teacher of the law or worker of miracles, not just a story teller who played with children. The historical Jesus was executed by the Roman state for the crime of rebellion, under the title "King of the Jews." He was a political figure, proclaiming a new way of life, for us to live out here and now in our lives and on this planet. "Heaven" was not a place to go when we died, it was a promise for us to fulfill in our relationships with one another. The early church was so taken by the man and his message that he was divine. "All authority in heaven and on earth has been given to me." All authority, that of rabbis and prophets and kings, "has been given," it is an accomplished reality. "Therefore, make disciples of all nations." Again, all means all. "Baptizing them," welcoming them, accepting them, "in the name of the Father and the Son and the Holy Spirit," the God who creates, who redeems and who sustains, and "teaching them to obey," not just to know, but to do, "all that I have commanded you. And behold, I am with you to the end of the age." This age has an end, and there will be a new age dawning, an age where all are welcome, where all are equal, where all are accepted and loved. And it will be heaven on earth. God's loving will accomplished!

The Sermon on the Mount is edited by the author of Matthew to state fully and clearly Jesus' manifesto: the message proclaimed by Jesus of the building of a new way of living, a new community, family, kingdom, age, that would replace and overturn the old. It was rightly feared by those in power because it would have meant the loss of their power. It is a powerful message today, and one just as threatening to those who choose to live by power and domination. It is a message just as welcoming for the oppressed and suffering, just as empowering to those who see themselves as poor. It is a message as counter-cultural now as then, and in every culture and society. It is the Good News of the love of God breaking into human lives and societies, to accomplish God's loving will and establish God's loving relationship with all God creation.

## FINAL QUESTIONS

What have you most enjoyed in this study? What has been most challenging? What questions has it raised in your mind? What difference has it made? What do you see as coming next?

# READING LIST

Barclay, William. *The Gospel of Matthew*. The Saint Andrew Press. Edinburgh. 1959.

Brown, Raymond. *The Churches the Apostles Left Behind*. Paulist Press. New York. 1984.

_____ and John P. Meier. *Antioch and Rome: New Testament Cradles of Catholic Christianity*. Paulist Press. New York. 1983.

Cornwall, Robert D. *Ultimate Allegiance: The Subversive Nature of the Lord's Prayer*. Energion Publications. Gonzalez, FL. 2010.

Craddock, Fred. *The Gospels*. Abingdon Press. Nashville. 1982.

De Dietrich, Suzanne. *Saint Matthew*. SCM Press LTD. London. 1961.

Edwards, Richard A. *Matthew's Story of Jesus*. Fortress Press. Philadelphia. 1985.

Grayston, K. "Sermon on the Mount" article in *The Interpreter's Dictionary of the Bible, vol. 4*. Abingdon Press. Nashville. 1962.

Harvey, A. E. *The New English Bible Companion to the New Testament*. Oxford University Press and Cambridge University Press. 1970.

Hill, David. *The Gospel of Matthew*. Eerdmans' Publishing. Grand Rapids. 1972.

Hunter, A.M. *Design for Life: The Sermon on the Mount*. SCMPress LTD. London. 1965.

Kepler, Thomas S. *Jesus' Design for Living: 40 Mediations on the Sermon on the Mount*. Abingdon Press. Nashville. 1955.

Jarvis, Cynthia A. and E. Elisabeth Johnson, Editors. *Feasting on the Gospels: Matthew vol. 1.* Westminster John Knox Press. Louisville. 2013.

Johnson, Serman E. and George A Buttrick. *The Gospel According to St. Matthew. The Interpreter's Bible.* Abingdon Cokesbury Press. Nashville. 1951.

Jordan, Clarence. *The Cotton Patch Version of Matthew and John.* Association Press. New York. 1970.

Luccock, Robert E. *Preaching Through Matthew.* Abingdon. Nashville. 1980.

Schuller, Robert. *The Be Happy Attitudes: Eight positive attitudes that can transform your life.* Word Books Waco Texas. 1985.

Schweizer, Eduard. *The Good News According to Matthew.* John Knox Press. Atlanta. 1975.

Shinn, Roger L. *The Sermon on the Mount.* Abingdon Press. Nashville. 1962.

Terry, John A. *Sermons on the Be-Attitudes: Invitations to the Kingdom of Heaven.* CSS Publishing. Lima Ohio. 1997.

Wink, Walter. *Jesus and Nonviolence: A Third Way.* Fortress Press. Minneapolis. 2003.

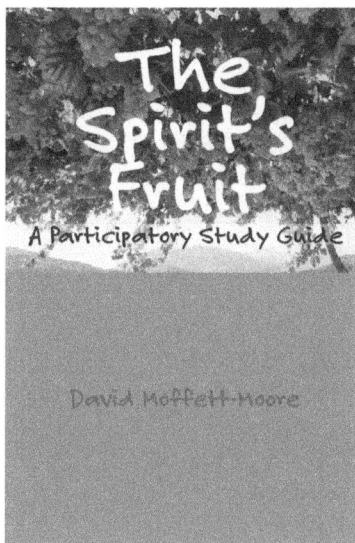

This is an eminently practical volume, yet one marked by solid study not only of the Letter to the Galatians but of the breadth of the Bible. Read this book – and bear the fruit of the Spirit!

The Rev. Steven M. Mullin
Presbyterian Church (USA)

Moffett-Moore shows the inadequacy of our contemporary public atheists and attempts to offer a twenty first century understanding of God. Readers of this book will gain new insights into the mystery of the Creator of Creation

Herold Weiss
Professor emeritus of New
Testament
St. Mary's College, Notre Dame
Author of *Creation in Scripture*

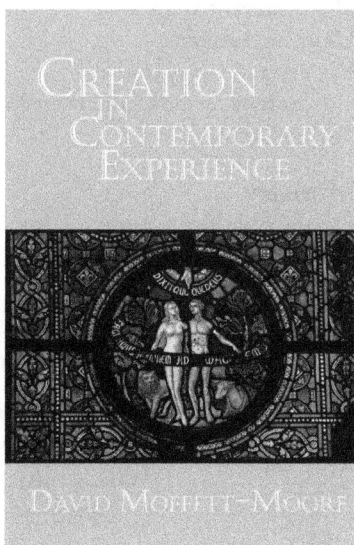

# MORE FROM ENERGION PUBLICATIONS

### Personal Study

| | | |
|---|---|---|
| Holy Smoke! Unholy Fire | Bob McKibben | $14.99 |
| The Jesus Paradigm | David Alan Black | $17.99 |
| When People Speak for God | Henry Neufeld | $17.99 |
| The Sacred Journey | Chris Surber | $11.99 |

### Christian Living

| | | |
|---|---|---|
| It's All Greek to Me | David Alan Black | $3.99 |
| Grief: Finding the Candle of Light | Jody Neufeld | $8.99 |
| My Life Story | Becky Lynn Black | $14.99 |
| Crossing the Street | Robert LaRochelle | $16.99 |
| Life as Pilgrimage | David Moffett-Moore | 14.99 |

### Bible Study

| | | |
|---|---|---|
| Learning and Living Scripture | Lentz/Neufeld | $12.99 |
| From Inspiration to Understanding | Edward W. H. Vick | $24.99 |
| Philippians: A Participatory Study Guide | Bruce Epperly | $9.99 |
| Ephesians: A Participatory Study Guide | Robert D. Cornwall | $9.99 |
| Ecclesiastes: A Participatory Study Guide | Russell Meek | $9.99 |

### Theology

| | | |
|---|---|---|
| Creation in Scripture | Herold Weiss | $12.99 |
| Creation: the Christian Doctrine | Edward W. H. Vick | $12.99 |
| The Politics of Witness | Allan R. Bevere | $9.99 |
| Ultimate Allegiance | Robert D. Cornwall | $9.99 |
| History and Christian Faith | Edward W. H. Vick | $9.99 |
| The Journey to the Undiscovered Country | William Powell Tuck | $9.99 |
| Process Theology | Bruce G. Epperly | $4.99 |

### Ministry

| | | |
|---|---|---|
| Clergy Table Talk | Kent Ira Groff | $9.99 |
| Out of This World | Darren McClellan | $24.99 |

Generous Quantity Discounts Available
Dealer Inquiries Welcome
Energion Publications — P.O. Box 841
Gonzalez, FL 32560
Website: http://energionpubs.com
Phone: (850) 525-3916

www.ingramcontent.com/pod-product-compliance
Lightning Source LLC
Chambersburg PA
CBHW031612040426
42452CB00006B/485